For Moritz and all our friends in Groß Glienicke
T.H.

For the Alexander family
B.T.

On the outskirts of Berlin,
beside the shore of a lake, there stands
a wooden house. It was built nearly a hundred
years ago by my great-grandfather.

I knew that my great-grandfather and his family had been
forced to leave this house when the Nazis rose to power, but I didn't
know what happened afterwards.

To find out, I visited Berlin in 2013 – and discovered the house empty,
abandoned, derelict. From there, I began to piece its story together …
a story that took me from the outbreak of the Second World War
to the rise and fall of the Berlin Wall, by way of four families.

This is that story: the tale of a house which
was, in its own quiet and forgotten way,
on the front line of history.

First published 2020 by Walker Studio,
an imprint of Walker Books Ltd
87 Vauxhall Walk, London SE11 5HJ

2 4 6 8 10 9 7 5 3 1

Text © 2020 Thomas Harding
Illustrations © 2020 Britta Teckentrup

The right of Thomas Harding and Britta Teckentrup to be identified as author
and illustrator respectively of this work has been asserted by them in accordance
with the Copyright, Designs and Patents Act 1988

This book has been typeset in Egyptian Extended

Printed in China

British Library Cataloguing in Publication Data: a catalogue record
for this book is available from the British Library

ISBN 978-1-4063-8555-7

www.walker.co.uk

The
HOUSE
by the LAKE

Thomas Harding

illustrated by

Britta Teckentrup

WALKER STUDIO
AN IMPRINT OF WALKER BOOKS

A long time ago, there was a little wooden house by a lake.
The house was built by a kind doctor and his cheery wife,
who wanted to live with their four children away
from the busy city.

They grew asparagus and lettuce, and collected eggs from their chickens. They played games in the garden and swam in the lake. At night, the doctor sat by the fire and read stories to the children. When the family was asleep, the house held their dreams.

The days went around like a wheel.

The sun rose, warming the walls of the house.

Woodpeckers *tap-tap-tapped* on the trees. Ducks floated through the reeds.

When the sun fell, starlight bathed the windows. This was a happy house.

But as the years passed and the children grew taller,
something was changing in the busy city.

One day, a troop of angry men banged on the door
and told the doctor and his family to leave.

The table and chairs were covered with sheets,
the shutters were closed, the doors were locked
and the angry men took the key.

The house was now alone.

A year went by – and then a new family came walking down the sandy path, carrying suitcases and instruments and love. The mother sang songs from the porch, the father played piano and the two boys built castles by the lake.

But slowly, their music changed. The boys started marching *click-click-click* on the wooden floors, and the mother took down the pretty metal gutters and gave them to a man who made guns.

Then a letter arrived. War was coming and the angry men wanted the father to fight for them.

So the family ran away, and cold air blew down the chimney once more.

Plane shadows kissed the roof,
and the cups and plates in the kitchen
rattled. The sky burned orange.

A husband and wife arrived from the city. They were friends of the
musical family, and the little lake house gave them shelter from the fear
and the fighting. It was a bitterly cold winter, but the house kept
them safe ...

for a while.

One chilly morning, the walls shook with the rumble
of tanks. Bullets struck the house, chipping its chimney
and breaking its windows.

The couple fled to the city, and once again the house was empty.

Spider webs grew across the windows and leaves piled on the porch. The paint on the shutters cracked and peeled. The house was abandoned and unloved.

*I*t stood empty for many long years – then, one day, a man with a fluffy hat came down the sandy lane. His two children shouted with delight and ran inside, casting light into the darkened rooms.

In spring, the man with the fluffy hat fixed the windows, the chimney and the gutters, painted the shutters and swept the porch.

In summer, his children rowed across the lake and had cake and ice cream.

In winter, they sailed boats across the marbled ice.

The house felt alive again: laughter in the hallway, sandy footprints on the floor, the smell of soup bubbling in the air.

One morning, the man with the fluffy hat woke to the growl of machines outside the house. Soldiers were building a giant wall through the garden. A wall with tall towers and bright lights and barking dogs.

The family hated the wall: it made everything grey. After school, the children had to work in the fields – there were no more trips across the lake. And the man with the fluffy hat spied on his neighbours.

Five, ten,
fifteen, twenty,
twenty-five
birthdays
passed by.
The children
became adults;
they left the
house and
had their
own children.
The greyness
hung for so long
that it seemed
like it would
never end.

Then, without any warning, the soldiers and barking dogs went away ...

and the man with the fluffy hat took a big hammer and knocked the wall down.
The sweet breeze from the lake blew into every nook and cranny of the house,
and his grandchildren jumped into the lake, whooping and splashing as they went.

The man with the fluffy hat grew old like the house. He found it harder and harder to take care of the ancient timbers and the wild garden – till one morning he didn't wake up, and the house was alone once more.

Its floorboards and doors were taken for firewood. Its windows were broken. Bushes and trees wrapped themselves around its tired walls. But still the house clung on.

Fifteen winters came and went.

Then a young man came down the sandy path. He took out a key, opened the door ... and saw at once that the house needed help.

He worked with the villagers to clean and clean. They cut back the bushes, fixed the broken floors and windows, and painted the house in bright colours.

Finally, the house shone like new.

The young man put a picture of his great-grandparents above the fireplace …

and the walls and the floors and the windows and the doors

remembered the kind doctor and his cheery wife.

Once again, the house by the lake was happy.

The HOUSE by the LAKE

THE DOCTOR AND HIS CHEERY WIFE

In 1927 my great-grandfather, Dr Alfred Alexander, built the house by the lake for his wife Henny and their four children. One of these children was my grandmother, Elsie, who called the house her "soul place".

The family spent their weekends at the house, providing an escape from their busy lives in the city. But the Alexanders were Jewish and in 1936, following the rise of the Nazis, they were forced to flee to London.

The house was then seized by the Gestapo (the Nazi secret police).

THE MUSICAL FAMILY

In 1937 the house was bought from the Gestapo by a music-publisher called Will Meisel, with his film star wife Eliza Illiard, for a quarter of its true value.

They lived there during World War II with their two sons, who became part of the Hitler Youth – a Nazi training programme for young boys.

The Meisels eventually fled to Austria in 1944 and didn't return to Berlin until after the war.

◆

THE HUSBAND AND WIFE FROM BERLIN

While he was in Austria, Will Meisel invited his creative director Hanns Hartmann and his Jewish wife Ottilie to take shelter at the house.

The Hartmanns fled just before Soviet forces occupied the village in April 1945.

After the war, a family called Fuhrmann also lived at the house for a time.

◆

The Man with the Fluffy Hat

From 1958, the house was rented by Wolfgang Kühne, his wife Irene and their two children. Wolfgang was a street-cleaner by trade, who also spied on his neighbours for the Stasi (the East German secret police).

On 13 August 1961, a fence was built between the house and the lake; later a concrete barrier was added. For nearly 30 years, this "Berlin Wall" divided East Germany from West Berlin.

Wolfgang died at the house in 1999,

and before long the house was abandoned — empty except for a vixen and her cubs.

◆

The Young Man

In 2013, I went to visit the lake house. I found the building overgrown by bushes, the windows broken and the inside full of broken furniture and rubbish.

I joined with members of my family and the local community, and together we cleaned up the house and restored it to its former glory.

Now renamed the **Alexander Haus**, the little wooden lake house has reopened as a centre for education and reconciliation.

For more information see **www.AlexanderHaus.org**